# IN THE
# NATIONAL INTEREST

General Sir John Monash once exhorted a graduating class to 'equip yourself for life, not solely for your own benefit but for the benefit of the whole community'. At the university established in his name, we repeat this statement to our own graduating classes, to acknowledge how important it is that common or public good flows from education.

Universities spread and build on the knowledge they acquire through scholarship in many ways, well beyond the transmission of this learning through education. It is a necessary part of a university's role to debate its findings, not only with other researchers and scholars, but also with the broader community in which it resides.

Publishing for the benefit of society is an important part of a university's commitment to free intellectual inquiry. A university provides civil space for such inquiry by its scholars, as well as for investigations by public intellectuals and expert practitioners.

This series, In the National Interest, embodies Monash University's mission to extend knowledge and encourage informed debate about matters of great significance to Australia's future.

Professor Margaret Gardner AC
President and Vice-Chancellor,
Monash University

# MICHAEL BRADLEY

# SYSTEM FAILURE: THE SILENCING OF RAPE SURVIVORS

MONASH
UNIVERSITY
**PUBLISHING**

Monash University Publishing
Matheson Library Annexe
40 Exhibition Walk
Monash University
Clayton, Victoria 3800, Australia
https://publishing.monash.edu

Monash University Publishing brings to the world publications which advance the best traditions of humane and enlightened thought.

ISBN: 9781922464781 (paperback)
ISBN: 9781922464798 (ebook)

Series: In the National Interest
Editor: Louise Adler
Project manager & copyeditor: Paul Smitz
Designer: Peter Long
Typesetter: Cannon Typesetting
Proofreader: Gillian Armitage
Printed in Australia by Ligare Book Printers

A catalogue record for this book is available from the National Library of Australia.

To Mia, Dina and Saxon, with deep thanks for trusting and allowing me to share their stories.

# SYSTEM FAILURE: THE SILENCING OF RAPE SURVIVORS

The events related here took place in 2020 and 2021. This is about what is happening today.

The following is an extract from Mia's police statement:[1]

Trent was taking me out to dinner for my birthday. He made his way down from the Central Coast on the train to my place. He told me he was drinking a long neck of beer on the train. He walked into my place, said hello and went straight to the fridge. He got a beer and walked onto the balcony to smoke a cone of weed. He also had a bong on the balcony.

I was getting ready in my room when he walked in and asked what I was wearing. He wasn't happy

1

with what I wanted to wear but I wore it anyway. I did change my shoes at his request. During this time, I had been drinking a glass of wine while he had already drunk three bottles of beer, smoked three cones of weed and whatever he drank on the train.

Around 8.00 pm, I had just finished getting ready and was about to walk out of my bedroom when I saw Trent standing at my bedroom door, basically blocking the doorway. We were standing face to face when he looked at me then looked down at his crotch. I felt like he was indicating for me to suck his penis.

I said, 'No, I've just got ready for dinner and the reservation's at 8.30.'

He said, 'I'm pretty hard.'

Trent unzipped his pants and took out his penis. I was getting pissed off at this point as it's my birthday dinner, he's already wasted and now he wants sex. I said, 'No.'

I tried to walk past him, when he put his hands on my shoulders. I'm 5 foot 4.5 inches tall and Trent is around 6 foot 2. He pushed me down with his hands on my shoulders and forced me onto my knees. I looked up at him and said 'What?'

He said, 'Be a good little girl for daddy.'

I remember him smiling like it was a joke. He put his hand on the back of my head and pulled my head towards his crotch. He started shoving his penis into my mouth. I couldn't even speak to tell him to stop as his penis was so far into my mouth and throat. He put both his hands behind my head and pulled it back and forth, multiple times. The force of his penis going into my mouth and throat was causing my eyes to tear and pain in my throat. I was gagging and felt like I needed to vomit. I put my hands on his thighs and tried to push myself away from him, but couldn't. He used so much force on my head that it caused one of my looped earrings to bend out of shape.

After a few minutes, I managed to push myself away from him. He did not ejaculate in my mouth.

I was crying and wiping away my tears and said, 'No, it's my birthday, I don't want to be servicing you today.'

He said, 'Pfft.'

I stood up and walked out of the bedroom. I felt rattled and in shock about what had happened. I walked down the hall to my dining table.

He followed behind me and once I was standing near the table, he pushed me onto it from behind, bent me over, pushed my dress up, moved my underwear to the side and inserted his penis into my vagina. I immediately froze and started crying as I didn't want to have sex with him. He thrusted his penis into my vagina for around one and a half minutes before ejaculating into me.

After he finished, I stood up, turned around and looked at him.

He said, 'What's wrong?'

I said, 'I told you I didn't want to do any of this.'

He said, 'Why are you crying?'

I said, 'Are you serious?'

He seemed a bit startled. After a minute or so he said, 'Oh baby I love you, I wouldn't hurt you.'

I said, 'Let's just go, we've got somewhere to be.'

We got an Uber to the restaurant. During dinner he was acting overly nice and charming towards me. We had a normal night out as if nothing had happened. He stayed at mine that night, he was very drunk and went straight to bed. We never discussed the incident again.

In her statements to the police, Mia described eight separate incidents of being raped by Trent. They occurred over a six-month period before Mia finally ended their relationship. A few months later, she made a report to the NSW Police Force.

Five months after that, Mia found herself alone on the footpath outside the Surry Hills Police Station, in her words 'left to walk home in a dissociative state, processing my shock and feeling like the world was crumbling around me'. She had just been informed that her case was closed. The police, without even interviewing Trent, had concluded that a prosecution wasn't likely to succeed. There had been no prior warning to Mia that this might be how it would end.

That it had come to this—as Mia later described it, a feeling of being used up, disregarded and discarded, her agency stripped away once more—reflected her status as another data point in the endless roll call of rape victims who the system has utterly failed. When it comes to rape, the exceptional is the norm.

~

I run a commercial law firm in Sydney, a place with a corporate client base and a human heart. My own practice, primarily in media and regulatory law, led me by a circuitous route to where I am now, lending time and support to survivors like Mia.

It began a few years ago with an introduction to Nina Funnell, who was working on an investigative piece for *New Matilda*, one of our clients. Nina is a journalist, a survivor, an advocate, and a deeply knowledgeable resource on the scourge of sexual violence in Australian society. Since then, I've worked in various guises with dozens of survivors. Their experiences are always unique but depressingly familiar. I have discerned some powerful consistencies in one critical aspect: the legal system's response to what they have suffered.

In April 2021, while the community was still processing the serial shocks of the Brittany Higgins and Christian Porter stories, the rape crisis at school level exposed by the efforts of Chanel Contos, and the almost inchoate rage demonstrated by the March 4 Justice rallies across the country, a ranking police officer spoke out in unusually clear terms. In an interview, then detective superintendent Stacey Maloney,[2] who had taken charge of the Sex Crimes Unit of the NSW Police Force two months earlier, explained the system failure over which she now presided:

> Sexual assault is endemic, and it is in our community. We're certainly not watering down the seriousness of it. But if we look at the data, we're not getting anywhere: nothing's being resolved, victims are still becoming victims, and offenders are still not understanding that the behaviour is not OK. That's the reality of it.[3]

For those who work in the system, and those who have encountered it, the fact of its brokenness is anything but a revelation. This has been recognised as a fact for a very long time. Looking at it objectively, as an outsider whose interaction with the system is tangential and, in a way, vicarious, I am struck by our illogical persistence in providing answers to what is clearly the wrong set of questions.

My purpose here is to explore the gulf between what our legal system offers and provides to victims of sexual violence, and what survivors who come to it seek and need.

~

Mia had met Trent through the dating app Bumble. After a few weeks of texting they got together for a drink in November 2019 and then started dating. Trent's work involved late-night shifts and a hard-drinking culture. In those first few months, while the relationship seemed to be going well, Trent's heavy drinking worried Mia because it tended to make him come down quite hard on himself.

And there had been one discordant incident: in December, while they were having consensual sex at her place, Mia realised that Trent was surreptitiously filming them on his phone. He seemed unfazed by her strongly stated objection, and he wouldn't show her his phone to confirm that he'd deleted the footage. Mia was unhappy about the incident but didn't pursue it.

By March 2020, Trent's drinking and increasingly frequent depressive episodes had become too much for Mia and she'd ended the relationship. There had been another serious issue as well: the first incident of rape.

It's at this point of the story where things start to get complicated, taking us away from the perversely comforting narrative of rape that we're taught as we grow up, centred on the phrase 'stranger-danger'—the violent sexual assault of a woman by a man she doesn't know, what is persistently called 'real rape'. Rape by an unrelated perpetrator of course exists, a horrific and appalling crime. However, research data consistently indicates that at least 80 per cent of rapes are committed by a perpetrator who is known to their victim.[4] The gap between the popular perception of rape and its more complex reality is an early clue. With familiarity comes the extremely problematic question of consent, creating hellish difficulties for prosecutors and intractable confusion for society—as Mia's story illustrates.

On the night in question, in March 2020, Mia was asleep in bed. It was 3.30 a.m. when her apartment buzzer sounded. She let in Trent, who was very drunk, stumbling and ranting. He looked like he had been crying. A few days earlier the same thing had happened. On that occasion, after raving to Mia about being afraid of losing his job due to COVID-19, and how he didn't have anything to live for, Trent had collapsed in a drunken stupor and slept it off. Now he really had lost his job.

Mia went to the kitchen and started making something for him to eat. As she bent over to retrieve a pan from a bottom shelf, she felt Trent behind her. She was relaxed, as he had never been violent with her. Trent pulled up Mia's dressing gown and tried to penetrate her from behind. That attempt failed, although he kept pushing the top part of her body down as he tried. Mia managed to break free and moved away. Trent followed, then pushed her against the stove, bent her over and sexually assaulted her again. Mia resisted and objected, loudly.

Trent retreated to the couch and resumed ranting, claiming that his life was over and he wanted to kill himself. Mia sat down next to him and tried to talk him down, but he was incoherently drunk and couldn't be reasoned with. Eventually she told him to go to bed where, as was the pattern, he eventually passed out, while she was set to endure another sleepless night of anxiety about his wellbeing.

Five days after this incident, Mia told Trent by text message that it was over. A month later she sent him another text: to wish him a happy birthday and check that he was okay. A month after that, they decided to give their relationship another go.

Many would comfortably proclaim that everything that happened subsequently was Mia's fault. There were already some early indicators of an abusive relationship: emotional manipulation, threats of self-harm, the breaching of boundaries and autonomy. The rape, of course, was a flashing red light. Still, she didn't leave. The reasons for that are well understood by experts and family and domestic violence victims and survivors, if not by a large section of the public.

This is not, however, a story about coercive control. The fact is that Mia, on whatever rationale, went back to Trent. And then there is this other fact, often overlooked: she hadn't consented to what he had done to her, and she hadn't consented to him doing it again.

After the pair had patched things up, the next couple of months were good. Trent cut down his drinking, started exercising, and got out of the industry whose toxic culture had been contributing to his personal problems. His mental health was looking up.

It was now early July 2020, a Sunday evening at Mia's place. Trent was watching golf on the TV in the living room. Mia was tired so she went to bed.

Shortly after, he came into her bed too and started watching the golf on his phone. Mia was now annoyed as well as tired and she rolled onto her side, facing away from him. Suddenly she felt his fingers pushing between her legs. The golf was still playing on his phone, which he held in his other hand. She objected. He laughed. A few minutes later he tried again. She slapped his hand away and told him to fuck off. He said, 'You love it.' She replied, 'Who the fuck would love that?'

Mia was furious about this incident but she let it drop, even when a week later Trent told her that he'd mentioned it to one of his mates, who 'thought it was hilarious'. Mia reacted by bursting into tears and walking away. They never talked about it again.

There was another complication: an embarrassing one. A bit before the golf incident, during the period when the relationship was in a good space, Mia and Trent had talked about their sexual fantasies. Mia had intimated that she had a sort of rape fantasy involving being tied up and dominated. She had very clear boundaries for this possibility in her head and she tried to lay them out explicitly to Trent. They included rules, safe words and the ability to release herself whenever she wanted. She articulated the kinds of acts that were entirely out of bounds, including being gagged.

Trent's response shocked her: 'Nah, I'm going to use duct tape to tape up your mouth. If I'm going to make it real for you and scare you, then all the other stuff has to be on the table too.'

Mia tried to get Trent to understand that she did not want it to be 'real' or scary, that it was role-play. She was open to experimenting, but only with clearly agreed boundaries and safety. Trent thought she was just being difficult and wouldn't shift from his enthusiasm for what he understood to be a rape fantasy. Mia concluded that they weren't on the same page and told him it wasn't going to happen. Trent brought the subject up a few times subsequently, but each time she shut him down.

The relationship staggered on. The couple were increasingly at odds and Trent's behaviour veered back towards the erratic as he started drinking more heavily again. It was the end of July when he raped her in her home on the night of her birthday dinner. Still she stayed with him, in circumstances that would appear all the more mystifying to an outsider. By September, the situation was spiralling out of control, with Trent frequently drunk and becoming verbally aggressive towards Mia. She was beginning to fear him physically.

One night, after a dinner with friends which Mia had terminated early because Trent was drunk and embarrassing her, they went back to her place and began having consensual sex on the lounge. Without warning, Trent began choking her, both of his hands around her neck, and he then grabbed Mia's hair and started forcing her to give him oral sex. She tried to push him away but he was too strong for her. He continued to use both hands to push violently on the back of her head until she couldn't breathe. Eventually the choking caused her to vomit all over her lounge.

Mia described what happened in her police statement:

I was crying while Trent was laughing. He grabbed me with his right hand on my throat and then slapped me across the face with his left hand, which caused me immediate pain. I didn't give him permission to slap me.

I said, 'How many times have I fucking told you to not slap me in the face!'

He laughed, then slapped me again.

I was so mortified and upset. I stood up and started cleaning up my vomit by removing the cover from the lounge. I was so frantic in trying to do this that I broke the zipper on the cover. After I cleaned up my vomit, I had a shower. Trent came into the shower and pretended like nothing had happened. We then went to bed.

Early the following morning, in her bed, Trent violently raped Mia again, initially with a vibrator and then with his penis, while grabbing her by the throat and pinning her down. She had warned him not to but he ignored her. He was watching himself in the mirror next to her bed. She used both hands to try to get his hand off her but failed. At this point, she couldn't speak or breathe. Eventually he was finished and got off her, lying on the bed next to her. Mia realised she was bleeding and went to clean herself. When she came back, his only comment to her was, 'Jeez I look pretty angry when I have sex.' Mia turned her back to him and went to sleep.

Three days later, the final rape occurred. The couple had met some of Mia's friends for drinks.

Trent was drunk and particularly obnoxious, calling Mia stupid and a 'fucking cretin' in front of her friends. She called the night off and they went home, where he passed out. Later that night, Mia was awoken by the sound of the balcony door opening; it was Trent, going outside to smoke a cone. She went back to sleep but woke again shortly after to find that he was in bed, penetrating her. This time she froze. It took a minute or so before he ejaculated, during which time Mia was unable to move or speak. The morning after this incident was the last time she physically saw him.

It was two more months before Mia began to realise that she had been the victim of violent abuse. Her first report was to her best friend. After some time in therapy, she made the decision to go to the police.

~

The crime of rape is ancient. The act itself we can safely assume has been occurring since the beginning of human evolution, and recognition of it as wrongful goes back as far as history records. That history and the etymology of the term 'rape' coincide in a critical and significant respect: why exactly rape was originally imagined to be a wrong at all.

The source of the word 'rape' appears to be the Latin word *rapere*, which means 'to snatch, grab, take away'. It emerged in England in the Middle Ages, deriving from the Anglo-French term *raper*, meaning 'to seize, abduct, carry off by force'.[5] Rape was a crime in ancient Rome, defined as the abduction of a female without the consent of the man who had authority over her, usually her father (if she was unmarried) or her husband. As Germaine Greer puts it, 'Once upon a time everyone knew what rape was; it was the stealing of a woman from the man or men who owned her.'[6] Rape was conceptualised in the first place as a property crime.

The conception of women as the property of men is hardly unfamiliar. Almost all cultures and societies have endorsed it and many still do. We therefore need not go further than recognising rape in the context of gender inequality; it's just a fact that the idea of women having equal personal rights to those of men is a very recent thing. Rape's origins are unconnected to sex, in the sense of the sexual act, although they are very much attached to sex as gender.

Until very recently, the law only understood rape as an offence committed by a man against a woman—a man could not be a victim of rape, and a woman could not be its perpetrator. What was always present in the definition of rape was a suggestion of violence, or more accurately a *violation*. However, the person violated was not the woman being raped but the man who possessed her. The residue of that unfortunate distinction remains today.

As the law evolved over time, the meaning of rape shifted from the act of forcible taking to the act of forced sex. English common law recognised rape as a crime from early on, defining it as the act of a male forcibly penetrating the vagina of a female. Consent— specifically the absence thereof—has been central to the law's construction of the crime of rape since it became an offence against a person.

All crimes consist of two essential elements: the actus reus and the mens rea, or the physical act and the 'guilty mind'. Originally, rape meant penile penetration of the vagina only. Anal sex, with consent or not, was deemed a crime against nature (that is, God) and dealt with rather more harshly for all concerned. Today the crime comprises a far broader range of physical sexual acts, and the question of whether or not the act happened is one of objective evidence; that is, although open to factual dispute, it is a yes/no question.

The mens rea or mental element is the tricky part, as it is in the criminal law generally. It refers to the mental state of the perpetrator, what they were thinking at the time of the act. The basic idea is that only a blameworthy person should be punished for his crimes. Breaking down the act of rape illustrates how the law became so fraught.

Two people have sex. So far, no problem. For it to be 'wrong', at least one additional element needs to be present. Originally, that element was force (the taking). As women became recognised as self-possessed persons, force gradually transmuted into its supposed inverse: the refusal of consent. Modern law is thus based on the notion that, if a person has sex but does not consent to it, then a crime has been committed. It has taken centuries for the assumption that force is an essential component of the wrongdoing to be excised, and that process is ongoing. In many societies, of course, force is still an essential element of the crime of rape.

In our own legal system, we continue to contend with the rape myth that women are capable of only two responses to a request or demand for sex: willing consent or violent resistance, both verbal and physical. The absence of resistance (submission) historically meant the same as consent, and today's criminal justice system still carries traces of that belief. The absence of consent is a deceptively simple thought, but it presents a problem that should be immediately troubling to lawyers: how do you prove a negative?

The law assists in some respects. It has created rules to say that, objectively, in some circumstances consent is deemed to be absent. Most obviously, children are incapable by law of consenting to sex (with many variations as to the age at which this cuts off and the grey areas around it). Likewise, a person whom the law considers incapable of making decisions for themselves (for example, a person in a vegetative state or with an extreme intellectual disability) is also unable to give consent and so it is always absent in their case. The problem lies with 'consenting' adults. The law says that, for there to have been a crime, consent must have been withheld by the victim. But what if the alleged rapist didn't know that or was honestly mistaken about it?

The famous English case of *DPP v Morgan* illustrates the problem. In 1973, Mr Morgan invited three of his friends over to his place and told them they could have sex with his wife. He explained that she was into a 'kink' that involved her feigning resistance, which they could safely ignore. Afterwards, Mrs Morgan said that she had not consented at all, and the three friends were charged with rape. The House of Lords ordered their acquittal, in doing so laying down a critical principle of law: that a conviction for rape is not possible if the defendant honestly believed that the victim was consenting to the act. More importantly, that belief did not have to be based on reasonable grounds. It could be 100 per cent wrong, perverse, unreasonable, untenable. But as long as it was genuine, there was no crime.

Lord Hailsham, one of the most eminent judges of all time, set out the basis of this principle in clear terms:

Once one has accepted, what seems abundantly clear, that the prohibited act in rape is non-consensual sexual intercourse, and that the guilty state of mind is an intention to commit it, it seems to me to follow as a matter of inexorable logic that there is no room either for a 'defence' of honest belief or mistake, or for a defence of honest and reasonable belief or mistake ... Since honest belief clearly negatives intent, the reasonableness or otherwise of that belief can only be evidence for or against the view that the belief and therefore the intent was actually held.[7]

This passage is one of the most important ever written about the law of rape. It is a piece of male logic par excellence, of course. His lordship saw rape in simple mechanical terms, as an act with an associated intent.

The first point to note is where the judge placed the absence of consent in his equation: within the actus reus, the physical act. He did not contemplate it having any relevance to the mens rea, the guilty mind. Consider what this phrase means: 'the prohibited act in rape is non-consensual sexual intercourse'. That's a question of fact, exclusively a matter for the prosecution to prove beyond reasonable doubt.

The other matter for the prosecution to prove is that the accused intended to commit the act; that is, he intended to have non-consensual sex. If he believed he had consent—that is to say, if he intended to have consensual sex only—then he couldn't have that guilty intent. Therefore, his *belief* (right or wrong, reasonable or not) is not a defence *to* the crime, but his *non-belief* is an essential component *of* the crime.

The law in Australia today is different from that laid out in *DPP v Morgan* in that reasonableness is now part of the equation. If the victim did not in fact consent to the act, but the defendant honestly believed that she did, he can still be convicted if his belief was not based on reasonable grounds. This means that a person can be the victim of a sexual act to which they objectively did not consent, but by law the person who perpetrated the act can be not guilty of rape, even in the absence of any dispute over the facts. Under today's law, Mrs Morgan's rapists could still be acquitted.

Here is the rub: the House of Lords treated rape as a crime of the perpetrator's body and mind, a question solely of what he did and intended to do. The law has carried that principle forward and it remains entrenched. In both practical and moral terms, this reflects the central controversy about sexual violence that continues to divide society today: the question of whose rights are paramount.

Rape is very often unclear, at least so far as each party is prepared to say. Very few men confess to rape; most of the time the allegation is hotly disputed. Putting aside the legal contest, at base is a conflict between two interests: the right of the accused to not be convicted without subjective guilt (a guilty mind) and the right of the victim to not be raped; that is, liberty versus autonomy. The two interests do not cancel each other out. It is entirely possible for a woman to be subjected to sexual intercourse to which she did not consent, in circumstances where the man who did it honestly and reasonably believed that she did, if we accept (as the law presently does) that he can reasonably hold that belief in the absence of affirmatively communicated consent.

Ultimately, what the law said is what it has always said: liberty takes precedence over autonomy. This maxim was laid down by the source of much of the authority for our common law, William Blackstone, in his four-volume *Commentaries on the Laws of*

*England* published in the 1760s: 'It is better that ten guilty persons escape than that one innocent suffer.' Benjamin Franklin later upgraded the number to 100 for American purposes, but you get the idea.

Our entire criminal justice system is predicated on guaranteeing the continuing liberty of the non-guilty, which underpins the presumption of innocence, the right to silence, and the burden on the prosecution to prove guilt of each element of the crime, beyond reasonable doubt. Which is all very well, except that it leaves autonomy in the dust. The right to autonomy—unqualified ownership and choice over what happens to one's own self—is placed by the law far beneath the right to liberty. Translated into the legal crime of rape, that means that the victim's own choice—to not have sex—is subsumed in the matrix of physical facts, which can be overridden if the perpetrator is not found to have had criminal intent.

In the most simple terms, according to the law, you can be raped without consequence.

This is the trap laid by the law of rape as it has been developed, by overwhelmingly male judges and more recently politicians (through legislation), over centuries. Whether you agree with its central proposition, that its wrongfulness is solely a function of the accused's mind and not the victim's, or you take the view that that is a regrettable artefact of millennia of misogyny, it is the law.

~

Of these matters of the law, Mia was completely unaware, as she was grappling with the question of whether or not to report her rapes to the police. Her mind was occupied by the growing realisation, assisted by therapy and friends, that she had been the victim of something horrific. As the reality of her experiences became clear, she was prompted to find a notepad she had been hiding in her home, in which she had recorded her thoughts and feelings about what Trent had done to her. Her own words broke over her like a wave of recognition.

Recognition is one thing; action is something else entirely. It is at precisely this point, when a survivor realises what they have survived, that they must by necessity reach out, for help. The question is: what help is at hand? For Mia, supported and guided by close friends, the only logical place to go was to the police. It's axiomatic, as an assumption, that the victim of a crime can, should and even must report it to the police. We are taught from childhood that the purpose of the police is to serve and protect; the corollary, supported by explicit admonitions and implicit narratives, is that we are obliged to enlist that service and protection as much as we are required to submit to it.

Generally in regard to non-sexual offences, which are broadly divided into crimes against the person and crimes against property, there's no controversy about the function of the police and our engagement with it. If your car is stolen, or a family member is killed, you call the police. It's natural to assume there's no difference when it comes to rape—it's a crime, analogous to assault but of a specific physicality, and the police must be called. We assume that rape survivors would want that too. Why wouldn't they? Consequently, they feel social pressure to report and the weight of disbelief if they don't.

For all the recognition that there is no validity to the ancient rape myths of late invention or falsified memories, social media (and, regrettably, sometimes mainstream media) can still fill up with posts along the lines of: 'If she really was raped, why didn't she report it at the time?' The imperative therefore operates both positively and negatively on survivors: it's their duty to go to the police, and it's a black mark against their credibility if they do not.

So Mia went to the police. Her initial experience was pleasantly surprising, as she described it. A friend had arranged, through a police officer he knew, for two detectives at a suburban police station to meet with Mia. They were supportive, encouraging and helpful. They explained to her that the case would have to be handled at a different station, but that they'd make sure she was looked after. They were true to their words, as Mia received a phone call from a female officer the next day. Detective Franks promised that she would stay with Mia's case through to the end. As she did.

A couple of days later, Detective Franks called Mia again and they had a long chat. She stressed to Mia that she believed her, listened empathically, even offered to come to Mia's home to take her statement. Mia felt good, strong and supported. Detective Franks, understanding, patient and kind, was on her side. She held Mia's hand, reassured her constantly.

Looking back, Mia says that she only persisted with the arduous interview process because of the detective's approach.

Mia went to the police station to begin the long, traumatic process of giving her detailed statement. This began in late November 2020 and wasn't concluded until March 2021. When Detective Franks went on leave for six weeks and handed the case to other officers to continue the investigation in her absence, Mia felt that they were cold and uninterested, and she elected to wait for her preferred officer to return. The two women spent many hours together in the interview room at the station, gradually piecing together the whole story. Mia's friends were interviewed, allowing them to give their accounts of what they'd observed and the disclosures Mia had made to them.

At this point, Mia felt that she had made the right choice in going to the police. She was in strong, supportive hands. She was being proactively kept up-to-date. And, unknown as yet to him, her perpetrator was going to be held accountable for what he had done. Even so, by early March, when Mia had completed her first statement and the investigation was ramping up, she began to have some doubts. Her first email to me explained:

I have recently reported an ex-partner for domestic violence/sexual assault and whilst I have been blessed with the support of an excellent female police detective, I feel like I am largely flying blind. I know if charges are laid that the case will be prosecuted through the DPP but feel a bit vulnerable in terms of what that means for me. The process has been gruelling so far and from what I understand, it will potentially get more challenging from here.

I am wondering if there is benefit in attaining legal representation for myself during this time, or if it is common for a victim to do so. I know the police are very focused on getting the best outcome for the case and not sure how much my overall welfare will be factored into the process and who, aside from myself, would then be tasked with advocating for me.

The issue looming largest in Mia's mind at this time was Detective Franks's request that she make what the police refer to as a 'pretext call'. This involves the complainant making a telephone call to the perpetrator, usually from a police station, while the police listen in and make a recording. The rationale for the pretext call is obvious: simply, the hope that the perpetrator will make an admission consistent with what the complainant has alleged.

Abusers are often inclined to admit to at least some aspects of their abusive behaviour, for complex and overlapping reasons. And the person most likely to be able to elicit an admission from them is their victim. Caught off-guard and unaware that the victim has already reported them, there is a decent chance that they'll say something self-incriminating.

For the police and prosecutors, this is gold. At the top of their wish list for evidence in a case of alleged rape is video footage of the crime—objective and unchallengeable, but extremely rare. Second-best is a confession by the rapist himself, followed by any admission he makes concerning any element of the crime. Third is third-party eyewitness testimony. Fourth is physical evidence (DNA, injuries consistent with the assault, implements and so on). Fifth is circumstantial evidence (to establish opportunity, motive or anything else consistent with guilt). At the bottom of the list is the evidence of the victim herself.

Rape almost never happens in front of witnesses or a camera (at least, not one that the police will ever get their hands on). The 'he said/she said' construct of proving rape—the public use of this expression should itself be a criminal offence—is pervasive but also, from the police's perspective, problematic. Thus, the police value a pretext call, and who can blame them. Mia's experience in this regard mirrors what I've consistently observed, that intense pressure is placed by police on survivors to agree to make such a call.

The problem with this is as simple as the reason the police want it. When I initially met Mia, her first question to me was 'Do I have to make the call?' The last thing she wanted was to hear her abuser's voice. It was still only a few months since she had finally escaped his reach, and she was nowhere near at peace with what she had suffered. She was vulnerable, uncertain and, according to my observation, not firmly in control of her own choices.

Detective Franks had told Mia that the pretext call wasn't compulsory, but that was not what Mia had heard. When the subject was first raised with her, Mia had visibly panicked, and the officer had backed off.

Nevertheless, Detective Franks raised it two more times, each time with greater emphasis. She told Mia it would make it easy for them to win the case, but without it, the allegations would be much harder to prove. The second time Detective Franks raised the issue, Mia had said no, she didn't want to do it. The third and last time, Mia felt the detective was talking about the pretext as if she had already agreed to do it and the previous conversations hadn't even happened. Maybe Detective Franks had forgotten that; perhaps she was confusing her case files.

Mia felt this as pressure—not overt or coercive, more a case of Hobson's choice, which is to say no choice at all. Either she relented and made the pretext call, which she had been left in no doubt was something the police badly wanted her to do, or she refused and the case might fail.

The impact of this experience on Mia wasn't difficult to predict. She was already captive to her gratitude to the detective who had taken her in hand, while still reeling emotionally and psychologically from the extensive abuse and violence she had been subjected to by Trent. She was in no position to make a clear choice.

That wasn't the fault of Detective Franks. She had a job to do, and that included pulling every lever available to her to deliver what she would assume to be everyone's desired result: a conviction for rape. It would be pointless to criticise the police for trying to obtain the best available evidence of guilt. But it would be even more ridiculous to blame Mia for not wanting to call her rapist. The risk, or rather near-inevitability, of re-traumatisation from doing so doesn't need to be proved. I haven't encountered a survivor who thought otherwise.

Here is the sharp-pointed conundrum: the strategy that will best achieve the universally acclaimed outcome in a rape case, is achievable only at a cost to the survivor of that rape and will compound the harm inflicted on her by the original crime.

The survivor should be excused for wondering why this is so. The paradox is easily identified and explained: it's just the natural consequence of the governing principles of our criminal justice system intersecting with the peculiarities of proof in a typical rape case. How else can guilt be established beyond reasonable doubt?

That is true, and it is what Mia was struggling to

understand when she came to see me. How was it that she was required to save her own case? I explained to her that she had no obligation to make the pretext call. The police were right, it was their best chance to build a watertight prosecution, and the likelihood of conviction would be much lower without it, but even so, that did not make it Mia's problem to solve.

During our first conversation, Mia learned something: that her rape case was not her case at all. To think the opposite is a common, I suspect uniform, misunderstanding. Survivors who report to police assume, quite naturally, that they will be the moving party in the prosecution of the crime committed against them. As I told Mia, that's not how it works at all. The moment a survivor goes to the police and makes a complaint, they become a piece of evidence. Their status does not rise above that until a conviction is achieved. Control of the process in the investigation, arrest and charging phase belongs exclusively to the police. From there through to the conclusion of the court case, it shifts to the director of public prosecutions. That is why, if you look at the law reports of criminal cases, the named parties are always the accused person and the state (in New South Wales, for example, it is the Crown, named *Regina*, or *R* for short). Literally, it is the state's case.

Part of the misunderstanding here arises from the popular belief that a rape case will not proceed unless the survivor 'presses charges'. That's not actually the law; the decision is in the hands of the police. It is true that, as a matter of practicality and policy, the police will almost never proceed with an investigation or prosecution without the survivor's willing involvement. The case can't be won without their evidence, so there wouldn't be much point. However, that is not the same as agency or control. At best, it's a veto right.

Every survivor I've met was surprised when they first realised how little actual power they had. This is consistent with the research into survivors' experiences: Judith Herman has noted in her work that survivors routinely said the 'single greatest shock' they experienced in the process was 'just how little they mattered', and that 'their marginal role in the justice system [was] a humiliation only too reminiscent of the original crime'.[8]

The pretext call, therefore, is not the problem but rather a minor symptom of the problem. On both sides of the pretext equation, heads are scratched with frustration and grievance. Why would a rape victim not want her rapist convicted, and therefore be prepared to take the practical steps required to best achieve that result? That is the natural perspective of the overworked and harried police investigator who is dealing with an ever-growing caseload of sexual assaults and trying to put at least some of the perpetrators behind bars. Meanwhile, for the survivor, there is mystification: how can the system be such that the pretext demand needs to be even considered, let alone made?

Talking to Mia, I confess that this was a lightbulb moment. Not that I'd discovered something that hasn't been well known and written about for a long time, but what I could see was a person caught in the middle of an impossible paradox.

A second question Mia had raised in her email to me was whether she should be engaging her own lawyer. She had come to this idea via her own consideration, not at anyone's suggestion or as a result of anything she'd read or seen. As she explained it, she was beginning to suspect that what the police were pursuing was something other than her personal interests. She appreciated that they were doing their best, with prosecution as their goal, but (as her email said) who was advocating for her?

Mia had raised with Detective Franks the possibility of getting her own lawyer and had met quite strong resistance. There was no need, the detective explained to her, as Mia herself faced no legal risks in the criminal case, the police and later the DPP would be on her side the whole time, and there was nothing a lawyer could do anyway apart from get in the way and complicate things to no good purpose. I've heard that response more than once from the police. In Australia, there is no tradition, policy or funding for rape survivors to have their own legal representation in connection with the criminal justice process—it just isn't done here, although it is in some places overseas.

The attitude of the police to the idea is unsurprising, because Detective Franks was right: lawyers would get in the way. The interests of the survivor and the police are different, not just subjectively but functionally. The police serve the state and, behind it, the public interest. That dictates a linear process of prosecution and punishment for crimes committed, regardless of their impact on the victim. For the prosecutor preparing the case for trial and then advocating it in court, there is an additional distancing factor: their primary ethical obligation is to justice. They are required to act impartially, to do what's fair—they must present the prosecution case and not inappropriately obstruct the defence in its quest to raise reasonable doubt. It is not their role to urge conviction on jury or judge at all costs.

In 2016, the Victorian Law Reform Commission recognised the gap between survivors' interests and the prosecution process. It formally recommended that a dedicated legal service be provided with government funding so that victims of violent crimes could have their own lawyers, whose role is to advocate for their rights and protect them; that is, to be on their side. The recommendation wasn't adopted.[9]

Mia put it to me in human terms: having made her complaint to the police, she was now starting to feel like she was sitting on a runaway train. She knew what the intended destination was, but she had no idea of the route the train was taking, and was understanding less and less of what was going on around her. She was on her way to being lost in the system.

~

At the outset of the police investigation, Detective Franks had discussed with Mia the possibility of taking out an Apprehended Domestic Violence Order (ADVO) against Trent. The detective had advised against it, so as not to tip him off that Mia had made a complaint and he was being investigated. Mia agreed that made sense.

Other police decisions were less explicable from her perspective. The second time she and I met, Mia was experiencing almost total confusion about the direction and progress of the investigation, despite maintaining her strong level of trust in Detective Franks. The detective had told Mia that she was planning to interview Trent's best friend Trevor, but she wouldn't tell Mia why, or what she was going to ask him. All Mia knew was that Trent had at one point told her that he had disclosed to Trevor the incident when he had assaulted her while watching golf, because he thought it was funny that she had objected. But why would the police talk to Trevor before speaking to Trent?

It was left to me to explain to Mia that she might never know. This was a basic home truth: not only was she not in control of the case, but the police could choose to conceal things from her. The fact that an investigating officer might not trust their complainant is, from the perspective of the police and lawyers, unremarkable. The investigation of an alleged crime may be initiated by a complaint, but that is evidence of nothing more than the existence of the allegation. The range of possibilities confronting the police include the allegation being true, but also that it is false. Motivation and memory are complex and changeable.

Among the thoughts occupying the detective, I explained to Mia, could be the risk of the investigation being interrupted or derailed by the complainant herself. There were almost certainly factual matters that Detective Franks knew about and was keeping to herself. To me, it sounded like the police had been tracking Trent's movements and were listening in on his calls. It would make logical sense, if the police spoke to Trevor about the allegations, that he might then immediately get on the phone to Trent. Then again, Trent might tell his mate something that could make the case for the police. Maybe. I didn't know for sure either way, but all a complainant can do is speculate.

A short time after this, Detective Franks updated Mia again, letting her know that she was obtaining a search warrant for Trent's mobile phone. Mia had told her that she and Trent had exchanged many text messages during their relationship, but Mia had deleted everything when she finally broke away from him. The detective also told Mia that she was no longer concerned about the pretext call. The search warrant would enable her to obtain material, including deleted files, from Trent's phone. She reassured Mia that with this material, along with a phone intercept which she mentioned in passing but didn't explain, 'We'll be fine'.

There was one more thing the police wanted from Mia: her medical records. Again, Mia was blindsided. Having been led to believe that Trent was close to being arrested, this further indignity seemed almost gratuitous. However, Detective Franks explained to Mia that, from the investigation's perspective, any evidence that Mia had reported her assaults to third parties would be very helpful. There was also a procedure available to protect her interests: sur-vivors are able to get free support from Legal Aid with respect to requesting and providing medical records to the police (this is the only form of publicly funded legal advice available to survivors in New South Wales).

Things were at least moving quickly now. It was 8 April when Mia found out about the assistance available from Legal Aid, which made direct contact with her six days later and immediately got on with contacting (on her behalf) her doctors and the rape crisis and domestic violence hotline services, to all of whom she had reported the assaults. Critically, none of the medical or hotline file materials would reach the police before 20 April.

Meanwhile, out of the blue, Detective Franks had also informed Mia that she was now going to be applying for an ADVO against Trent, to coincide with serving the search warrant, and the interim ADVO was duly issued on 12 April. Mia hadn't been consulted about this, so she was still feeling unsettled, but what was happening and what the detective was saying to her all seemed to point to an imminent arrest. Mia emailed Detective Franks to thank her for sorting out the ADVO: 'I really appreciate all the support you've provided. This certainly gives me peace of mind. I'm so relieved I could cry.'

The next contact Mia had with Detective Franks was a week later, on 19 April. In a short email following up on the Legal Aid aspect, the detective asked Mia if she was 'able to come in at a time that suits you to discuss the matter?' Mia replied in the affirmative, adding: 'Is everything ok? Anxiety is a bit high at the moment so wanted to know what I'm preparing for, if anything.' Detective Franks was equivocal in the response she sent six hours later:

> In relation to tomorrow's meeting, I wanted to discuss with you the outcome of the enquiries I've conducted and the status of the investigation. I hope you can try to keep busy and not think too much into tomorrow's meeting. In saying that, I know it's easier said than done. See you tomorrow.

Mia went to the police station after work on 20 April. She immediately knew that something had changed—Detective Franks's manner was completely different from how she had been throughout her previous dealings with Mia. As Mia described it, this time there was no eye contact, no niceties, with Franks imparting what she wanted to say with a halting, rambling delivery.

The detective launched into a long explanation of what she had been doing: how she'd executed the search warrant to get Trent's current and old phones and his laptop, how it was clear that he wasn't a 'good person', how 'extremely manipulative' of Mia he had been. She could see that Mia had been reticent about his sexual demands, and she'd seen how much pressure he'd put on her to submit.

Then it came: 'There's a lot between you, a lot of text messages. It doesn't look good for you.'

It doesn't look good for you … It's so often in the unconscious, the unprepared choice of words, where we find both truth and meaning.

Bear in mind, as Mia had been painfully learning over the preceding months, this was not her case or investigation. The exercise of choice belonged to the police. Mia had been progressively relegated to observer status, as survivors routinely are by the imperatives of the process. But now it wasn't looking good *for her*. The words hit Mia like a hammer blow.

The impact of those two small words really does justify a pause to reflect. They could only make sense in a context of suspicion and potential blame. It seemed that Mia was standing accused of something, and she was being told that her defence wasn't looking good. She was at risk of, what exactly? Embarrassment? Shame? Condemnation?

The detective pressed on: 'The two of you talked about a sex tape, and now you're accusing him of making one. The texts where you're talking about a rape fantasy, that aligns with the final incident when you were asleep.'

Mia, struggling for words at this point, said, 'This is really humiliating.'

Detective Franks replied, 'Yes, I'd be embarrassed too.'

Mia was crying now, as the detective went on: 'The jury is going to lap that up. I wouldn't put you in front of a barrister, because he's going to tear you apart.'

Mia wasn't able to respond; the walls were closing in on her. However, the detective continued to make her point heard: 'You don't want all this stuff seen by everyone. And the jury won't believe you. It becomes a "he said/she said" thing, and the jury just won't believe it.'

To Mia, the detective seemed frustrated, complaining to her that she had gone above and beyond for her, done more than anyone else would have.

Then the death knell: *The case is closed.* It was repeated three times, to make sure Mia had heard it.

Detective Franks's tone shifted once more, lighter now: 'He is clearly a bit of a sex pest. I'm going to have a good chat with him tomorrow when I return his phone and laptop, about how he treats women.'

Mia could only think, *I have to get out of here.*

The detective walked her out of the police station, saying that she was really sorry Mia didn't get the result she wanted. Mia was in full flight mode now, struggling to get her bearings. Detective Franks left her to make her own way home.

Mia told me later that, if she had not gathered her own supports around her during the arduous investigation process but instead had been solely reliant on the police, she may well have killed herself following her final meeting with them.

~

The next day Detective Franks emailed Mia, making no reference to what had happened the day before but updating her on two things: that she had returned Trent's property and 'had a good talk to him about everything' while making sure he deleted every photo and video of Mia, as well as their entire message history, from his phone; and that the ADVO hearing had been adjourned and it was possible that Trent might be contesting it.

Mia emailed me the same day to arrange a meeting, but she soon postponed it for a week as she was unable to do anything at all. Five days later, she wrote at length to Detective Franks, setting out with remarkable clarity what she had experienced and how she had been left. This is part of what she said:

> I am not writing with an expectation for the case to be reopened. You made it very clear that was not an option. I am advocating for myself as a survivor and highlighting how we can be re-traumatised by an experience like this. There aren't sufficient words to explain how vulnerable and exposed I've felt throughout this process; how it has taken every ounce of fight I had in me to go down this path, to wake up every day and try to function like a normal human being when all I feel is fear and panic; and how difficult it's been to maintain grace and dignity whilst sitting with the anger of what happened to me.

Consider this my impact statement.

I understand from an evidence perspective, the information in those text messages adversely affected how compelling I would be as a witness. I also understand that in the eyes of the law, [non-]consent would be difficult to prove, given there was written evidence of discussions being had between Trent and me.

What I also know to be true, is that in reality, this isn't how consent works. There may be text messages but there were also subsequent conversations had, with me being very clear about not being comfortable to participate. Regardless, one has the right to change one's mind at any stage and saying no is enough for consent to be removed.

Just because sexual assault cannot be proved in court, it doesn't mean it didn't happen. I know what happened to me and am living with the trauma of it every single day.

The text messages, for Detective Franks, had clearly been the deciding factor against prosecution. In fact, in the end she had not even attempted to interview Trent before making the call to close Mia's case.

Nor had the detective considered, because she hadn't even seen, any of the evidence from Mia's medical files or the reports she had made to the crisis hotlines. This evidence was contemporaneous, graphically detailed and compelling. It wasn't discounted—it wasn't even reviewed.

Mia told me that the detective was right about the volume of messaging between her and Trent, and that it had included considerable sexual content. There had been conversations about a rape fantasy, as the couple had also had in person, and suggestions of acts to which Mia might agree to submit. It was open, unsubtle, and plainly it was never intended that anyone else see it.

And, Mia was perfectly willing to concede, it was a complication. Unsurprisingly, at least it seemed to her, because she had been in an intimate relationship with Trent that included sometimes unconventional sex, the particulars of consent/non-consent were not as straightforward as the police and prosecutors would prefer. Probably it would be challenging for a jury to navigate as well, possibly even enough to find a reasonable doubt, on the law as it stands.

However, what had happened had happened, and Mia knew in her own mind that she had been repeatedly raped. She went on in her email to Detective Franks:

My multiple assaults were not due to confusion regarding consent. He simply did not care and chose to ignore the fact I was not a willing participant. It's not a stretch to consider a 'sex pest', as you called him, not being willing to respect physical boundaries, even when it's been made abundantly clear. I don't believe having 'a good chat' with a 'sex pest', who has a history of violating boundaries, would have had any meaningful impact. In fact, I think he'd be feeling emboldened to continue as he pleases, as there have been no repercussions for his behaviour.

On this, according to the experts, Mia was right. Detective Franks's blithe assurances that, despite the fact that Trent would get away with what she herself had repeatedly professed was rape, she could achieve something both useful and comforting to Mia by having 'a good chat' with him, reflected an almost absolute failure of understanding.

Rape, need it be repeated, is an act of power and control. Where it occurs in the context of a relationship that involves coercive abuse, that is all the more obviously the case. To put it indelicately, Trent was not lacking access to consensual sex with Mia. Having been told that there were boundaries, which he did not like, he chose to cross them anyway.

Trent was not a sex pest. He was a manipulative, aggressive predator. While the cliched old-school policing technique of 'having a chat' may even today have some currency in convincing a wayward youth to return to the straight and narrow, it was never relevant to rape and never will be. That Detective Franks—a specialist sexual assault investigator—thought it might help or, worse, that it might make Mia feel better, is truly disturbing in 2021.

Mia's note continued:

I went into this process knowing how awful it was going to be. I also knew that the evidence may not work in my favour and even though I was terrified, I proceeded anyway. No one would willingly expose themselves to this process for any other reason than to be heard and believed. Despite these odds, I forged ahead and shared the most devastating and private details of my assaults, including agreeing to provide access to my medical and counselling records because I have nothing to hide. But in the end, those records weren't even reviewed.

I trusted you with this information, but what I took from our discussion was that you had already made a judgement call as to his guilt (or in this case a lack thereof), based on our chat history. In your haste to give him the benefit of the doubt without questioning him, you seem to have forgotten that in addition to violent sexual assault, there was a history of coercive behaviour. He also emotionally and psychologically abused me, but the system isn't designed to give me justice for that either.

Consequently, after our meeting, I left feeling abandoned at a critical juncture. I felt slut-shamed, like I had somehow invited it and was to blame. It felt like you were incredibly frustrated with me, that I had been wasting your time and worst of all, that you no longer believed me.

I'm wondering if that was what you had intended to convey to me, or I've somehow misinterpreted the interaction? Having built a relationship with you over the past few months, I'm inclined to believe that it wasn't intentional, but it has caused immeasurable damage, nonetheless. I cannot make sense of what happened, particularly when it was in stark contrast to how safe, believed and protected I'd been made to feel throughout the investigation.

I tried to clarify the seriousness of what you wanted to discuss prior to our meeting on Tuesday. Even though you are acutely aware of the impact this has had on my mental health, there was no indication as to the significance of the update. From a duty of care perspective, I should have been told to bring a support person along, due to the enormity of the news, rather than be left to walk home in a dissociative state, processing my shock and feeling like the world was crumbling around me.

There are women I know who were ready to come forward to report their own experiences of assault and abuse, based on how my case was being handled in the preceding months. I doubt they'd feel safe enough to do so now, having seen the effect this outcome has had on me. I am honestly shattered about this.

With the status of the ADVO still uncertain, I am unable to put this ordeal behind me and move on. I am hoping it will be the final indignity I have to suffer regarding this matter, and it doesn't get dragged out further than Wednesday. I just want to feel safe and be afforded the space to find some peace.

In the end, Detective Franks (or someone higher up—Mia will never know what Franks really thought personally) had concluded that this was a dead case. She should be credited with sincerity and being concerned to not subject Mia to what would undoubtedly have been a horrible experience in the witness box, and the very real prospect of an acquittal for Trent.

While the state has no corporate interest in a survivor's wellbeing, other than in the most abstract sense, the individual police officers and prosecutors who work with her would be inhuman if they didn't care. Exactly as Mia has pointed out that no survivor would subject themselves to the criminal justice process for other than good reasons, we can assume that nobody would choose to work in the field of prosecuting rape if they were indifferent to its victims.

So, at its core, this is not a failure of humanity, much as one can legitimately criticise the appallingly clumsy way in which Detective Franks brought Mia's case to an end. Human failure is not system failure. The terrible denouement to Mia's journey through the police process was only a reflection of the fact that she had been pursuing a chimera all along.

~

With all the facts of Mia's case revealed, it is easy to see that it was never going to be the simplest prosecution to pursue. In the face of Trent's (assumed to be inevitable) denials, the public prosecutor would have had to contend with all the most problematic features of our current rape laws.

Rape, or sexual assault as it is referred to by the NSW *Crimes Act*, requires proof beyond reasonable doubt of these elements by the prosecution:

- the accused had sexual intercourse (penetration or cunnilingus) with the complainant

- the complainant did not consent
- the accused knew the complainant did not consent, or was reckless as to whether they consented, or had no reasonable grounds for believing that they consented.

'Consent' is defined as free and voluntary agreement. The law says that consent is not present when the complainant has no opportunity to give it because they are unconscious or asleep, or if they give consent but only because of threats of force or terror. In addition, absence of consent can be found where the complainant was intoxicated or their consent was given because of intimidatory or coercive conduct, or a non-violent threat. Finally, these days, the law explicitly provides that a complainant who does not offer physical resistance to the assault is not solely for that reason to be regarded as having consented.

Had Trent been arrested and charged, and assuming he had admitted that all the sexual acts alleged by Mia had occurred, but claimed that they were consensual, then the prosecution would have had to prove that Mia did not consent. It would then also have to convince the jury that Trent, despite his denials, knew she wasn't consenting, or didn't care. Or—if he honestly believed that he had her consent—that he didn't have any reasonable basis for holding that belief.

Confused? Try being a judge making sure all of that is straight in the minds of twelve jurors.

It's not my purpose, however, to dig deeply into the problems with the legal test for rape and how it might be reformed; that is a very big conversation around the edges of which we just keep tiptoeing.

There are a couple of critical things to note here. One is where the burden of the law sits. Technically, of course, it sits on the prosecution. But in real terms, in the meat of the matter where the jury's minds will be concentrating, the burden is laid at the feet of the victim. That links directly to the second critical factor: what is consent? The law defines it as free and voluntary agreement, but missing from that equation is communication. Therefore, in legal terms, consent is a quantity that exists entirely within the confines of the complainant's mind.

The 'affirmative consent' model currently being advocated (so far, the only Australian jurisdiction to have adopted it is Tasmania) seeks to overcome this problem via a legal formula that says consent which is not positively communicated is not consent at all. That would close the gap that Mia clearly identified: the likelihood in a case like hers that, although she did not consent to what Trent did, he would still be acquitted because there was enough doubt about what he reasonably believed.[10] But the gap would remain wide enough even then for Trent to have a good chance of escaping any consequences. While the law has been progressively reformed over the years to restrict the scope for defendants to 'slut-shame' complainants (for example, they can no longer be cross-examined about their prior sexual history) and to combat persistent rape myths (such as that 'real' rape victims always physically resist), the playing field remains anything but even.

Mia could expect to be questioned aggressively about her rape fantasy: what she said about it to Trent, what she agreed to or hinted she might agree to, whether he could have been forgiven for thinking she was inviting him to dominate her even when she was fighting back. Their messaging history would have been exhaustively trawled, and the coercive control features of their relationship glossed over in favour of a defence narrative of a tempestuous and sexually adventurous affair.

Plenty of people would read Mia's account and say that the police were right to close her case. Too hard, too messy, maybe she's lying, perhaps he genuinely mistook her signals. Who wants to look that closely into the bedrooms of other adults? What we see there is terminally confused.

While Mia knows exactly what happened to her and would be justifiably upset by the righteous judgementalism of strangers—not to mention that of the police officer to whom she had entrusted her mortification—she knew all along that obtaining a conviction wouldn't be easy. Which begs the question we began with: why put herself through it at all?

~

Another of my clients asking herself the same question was Dina, after the police told her that they were closing her rape case without laying charges.[11]

Dina is a musician who is based in another country. In 2019, as part of a multi-country tour, she was in Melbourne, sharing an Airbnb house rental with the tour promoter and Terry, a fellow musician from overseas. One afternoon, when they were alone at the house, Terry came on to Dina. It started with a request for a hug, then to lie down, and, via an extremely confused (according to Dina's police statement) succession of events, it ended in several acts of rape. She went to hospital the same day, where she was forensically examined, and she made a detailed statement to police two days later.

As becomes obvious after you've read enough survivor accounts, and in complete contrast to the popular understanding, the dynamics of rape are rarely straightforward and frequently an absolute mess. It shouldn't surprise or confound us, but it does. Dina had submitted to quite a lot of what Terry wanted, for complex and, on her reflection, mystifying reasons. Dina is small; Terry is an enormous man. She was physically scared of him, sexually inexperienced and discomfited by his forceful, uncompromising insistence. She was also fond of him, although not attracted to him. When he started moving on her, she tried to control the situation by giving in a little while maintaining a boundary, but it kept slipping.

Her speedy descent into a state of frozen fear left her close to helpless.

Nevertheless, Dina told Terry at various points that her vagina was 'not for you', that 'I don't know what you're doing but I'm not comfortable with it', and to 'stop it'. She used tactics like hiding in the bathroom pretending to be using the toilet for an extended period, and claiming she needed to do work. Ultimately she submitted to the final sexual act, her fear by this point of being repeatedly raped flooding any other possibilities.

Reading Dina's statement, one is struck by her honesty (the idea that anyone would ever want to concoct such a messy story is just bizarre) and the sheer enormity of the emotional storm she experienced while simultaneously being physically and sexually monstered by Terry. At one point in her statement, she recalled that: 'My brain was totally not processing, I was screaming in my head, "What the fuck is going on??"'

Terry, no doubt, would have recalled the incident differently, but he was never asked. Victoria Police, following Dina's report to them, commenced an investigation in November 2019. Not much seemed to happen—Dina heard very little from the officers involved and became increasingly frustrated with the apparent lack of progress on her case. Then, in January 2021, after fourteen months of near-silence, Dina received a phone call and a brief, exceedingly spare letter from the police:

> Your report has been fully investigated.
>
> As per our telephone conversation, a decision has been made to not proceed with charges.
>
> The reason for this is that there is insufficient evidence to proceed to trial.

I arranged a conference call with Dina, the investigating detective and that officer's superior, to find out what lay behind that uninformative communication. The senior officer explained that he had decided the case wasn't strong enough to proceed with, giving us the benefit of his summation of the difficulties faced by police investigating sex crimes: 'The investigation of sexual assaults is notoriously difficult. In a lot of cases, it's a situation of two people only, no witnesses, where we have the complainant's account and the accused's account. It's a "he said/she said" situation.'

That is all undoubtedly true. It is certainly time for police officers to resist using the deeply offensive 'he said/she said' throwaway line on the misplaced assumption that it will somehow comfort survivors whose experience of being raped the police are in the process of dismissing. However, the central point is unarguable: under our criminal law, it is vanishingly hard to get a rape case up. And Dina's case was far from the easiest prospect.

Still, Dina had been violently raped.

~

It is possible to be critical of the police officers' decisions in Mia and Dina's cases to not make an arrest. Indeed I am, although by far the greater concern is that the police appear not to have been at all trauma-informed—working from the understanding that a complainant is likely to be experiencing trauma, which may impact them, their emotions and their relationships with others, and that they are vulnerable to triggering events and circumstances—and were clearly labouring under the influence of ancient rape myths that supposedly have been erased from our legal institutional structures. They obviously had no idea how to protect the psychological and emotional wellbeing of their complainants. That is very disappointing but, in my experience over the past few years, unremarkable.

If the police had chosen differently, and Mia or Dina found herself moving to the next stage of the criminal justice process, would that (for her) be any better? We are back in the territory of the underpinning social assumption that everyone wants rapists to be prosecuted and punished as an end in itself, especially their victims. However, survivors whose cases have gone the whole distance don't necessarily agree.

Saxon Mullins, whose case catalysed the affirmative consent movement in Australia, has been open about her own ambivalence. This illuminating exchange appears in Louise Milligan's book *Witness*:

Seven years down the track, I ask Saxon to reflect on her own experience of the criminal justice system.

'My experience of the criminal justice system from the view of the survivor was so awful,' Saxon says. 'People have asked me if I'd recommend going to trial or not, I don't know the answer. I have no idea of the answer. Because it's such a horrible event.'

She adds that when 'someone says it has to be blunt and brutal, I kind of laugh with tears in my eyes. Because I think to myself, "You really don't know what blunt and brutal is."'[12]

Saxon makes a deep impression when you meet her, and her words deserve the weight that they have increasingly been carrying. Her rape case is notorious. Briefly, she was eighteen and on her first big night out in Kings Cross in 2013 when she was allegedly anally raped in a laneway behind the Soho Club by the owner's son, Luke Lazarus. Lazarus was convicted of sexual assault by a jury but that was overturned on appeal. After a second trial before a judge only, he was acquitted. That decision was also successfully appealed, this time by the Crown, but there would be no third retrial. The appeal court decided that, Lazarus having already served ten months in prison, it would be unfair to allow the case to go any further. By then it was 2017.

The bare time line is a daunting enough prospect for a survivor contemplating following Saxon's path. The sheer awfulness of her experience of the justice system could not but dissuade anyone from wanting to, even if a successful outcome could be guaranteed (which, obviously, it cannot).

A passage from Saxon's cross-examination by Lazarus's barrister during the first trial gives a small taste of what survivors can expect. Saxon was adamant in her evidence that she had told Lazarus to 'stop' during his attempts to penetrate her anally from behind. The defence barrister took her to the statement she had made to the police the day after the alleged rape:

> 'You say here, "I think at one point I told him to stop"?'
>
> 'That's correct.'
>
> 'Well, you weren't certain were you?'
>
> 'I was, yes.'
>
> 'Well, you don't say, "I told him to stop", do you?'
>
> 'That's correct.'
>
> 'You say, "I think at one point I told him to stop"?'
>
> 'That's correct.'
>
> 'They're very different meanings in English, those phrases, aren't they?'
>
> 'I suppose so, yes.'[13]

The judge who acquitted Lazarus did so because she didn't believe Saxon's version of what happened in the laneway, preferring Lazarus's evidence. Critically, she didn't accept that Saxon had at any time said 'stop', partly because she thought Saxon's evidence about the physical nature of the intercourse was unreliable, partly because of Lazarus's good character, and partly 'based on the application of common sense'.[14]

Bear in mind, it was not disputed that Lazarus and Saxon had had anal sex, nor that Saxon had as a fact not consented to it. However, Lazarus said that he honestly believed that he had her consent, so the prosecution had to prove beyond reasonable doubt that he had no reasonable grounds for that belief. The judge believed that, 'in her own mind', Saxon had not consented, but her actions had communicated the opposite to Lazarus. His version of what she said and did was believed; Saxon's testimony, of her confusion, drunkenness, her freeze response when Lazarus's tone turned from charming to demanding, the judge found unconvincing.

Significantly, the judge placed heavy reliance on evidence of contemporary morality, which she drew from a witness for the defence: another young woman who had been in a relationship with Lazarus a year before the alleged rape. That woman said she had withdrawn her consent for a sexual act just before it was about to happen, and Lazarus had immediately acquiesced. The witness also educated the judge about young people's attitudes to anal sex: 'I know for me, I've had anal sex with guys knowing them just that night, and there was consent. So whether or not, if there was consent there, then I have no problem with it.' The judge, referring to this evidence, said, 'I accept that by that she meant whether the accused believed there was consent.'

The prosecution had argued that the physical circumstances of the intercourse between Lazarus and Saxon had excluded any possibility of him reasonably believing it to be consensual. The judge rejected this argument,

> particularly so when looking at the event together with the evidence of the young people who gave character evidence and especially the young woman to whose evidence I have just recently referred. Their evidence allowed some insight into the contemporary morality of that group of young people.[15]

That is to say, a group of young people of which Saxon was not a member. Nevertheless, having entered their world, drunk herself silly and spent hours bouncing between nightclubs, she had left herself at the mercy of the 'contemporary morality' of young people at 4 a.m. in Kings Cross.

Saxon, unlike generations of rape survivors preceding her, was not judged an unmeritorious victim by virtue of being too forward in her personal behaviour, but rather by lagging a little too far behind. Just like them, she should have known better than to place herself where she did, in the state she was in. She didn't consent to being raped, but she didn't communicate that clearly enough and the result was on her.

~

The experts are unanimous on the failure of the criminal justice system to serve the needs and interests of survivors. Judith Herman summarises it well:

> The legal system is designed to protect men from the superior power of the state but not to protect women or children from the superior power of men.

It therefore provides strong guarantees for the rights of the accused but essentially no guarantees for the rights of the victim. If one set out by design to devise a system for provoking intrusive post-traumatic symptoms, one could not do better than a court of law.[16]

Rape & Domestic Violence Services Australia, a peak non-government body that provides frontline counselling services, including the NSW Rape Crisis Centre, describes the experience of survivors as one 'characterised by uncertainty, delay, distress and, very commonly, re-traumatisation'.[17]

What do the police think? Not many senior officers are prepared to speak with quite the frankness of detective superintendent Stacey Maloney, but there isn't much willing defence of the system either. Appearing in March 2021 before a NSW parliamentary hearing into the circumstances of the NSW Police Force's handling of the rape allegation against Christian Porter that had been made to it by a since-deceased woman, NSW Police Force Commissioner Mick Fuller was guarded but pointed. Explaining why the police as a matter of practice do not pursue allegations without the alleged victim's active participation, he said:

> Now, whether that is right or wrong, they are certainly things that we are looking at at the moment with a whole broader range of things around the journey for victims into the justice system, particularly around sexual assault and historical sexual assault.[18]

Fuller noted that police were able to proceed on only 10 per cent of the sexual assault complaints they received, and convictions were secured in only 10 per cent of those.

> The issue of consent, it's been one of the struggles for juries, judges and magistrates, and it is a real issue that's playing out today. I think there needs to be a line drawn in the sand about what consent is, and I think there needs to be a better criminal definition around that.[19]

Giving evidence at the same hearing, NSW Police Minister David Elliott was more blunt: '[W]hen I read some of these briefing notes that I see about young women, coming through police channels, that have been assaulted, it's quite clear that society has failed.'

And the prosecutors? I spoke with an extremely experienced public prosecutor who is second in command of the sexual crimes unit at one of Australia's offices of public prosecutions. Her reflections, from deep inside the institutional beast, are damning. 'I'm sorry but I have no faith in the system,' she says. 'It doesn't do what we imagine it does. Sexual violence by its nature is a violation of autonomy. All we do is violate it further. We take people's stories and they become our property. We need a complete reimagining of how we respond to this social ill.'

The statistics of failure are increasingly well known but staggering all the same. According to the most recent Australian Bureau of Statistics figures, for 2016, 639 000 Australian women had experienced a sexual assault by a male in the previous ten years, 200 000 in the preceding twelve months. One in six adult women have been raped at least once since they were fifteen.[20] The same proportion of survivors (one in six) went to the police about their rapes. The figures become harder to verify the further you trace them through the criminal justice process—conviction rates are low (around 40 per cent), but of course only a small minority of reported rapes are prosecuted at all, and police reports in turn represent only a small minority of actual assaults.

In reality, we're looking at less than 10 per cent of the rapes reported to police resulting in a conviction, and some data indicate a rate of 3 per cent or even lower (indeed, if the numbers Fuller gave the parliamentary hearing are accurate, it's 1 per cent). It is not in any sense an exaggeration to say that, overall, when a woman has been raped, the likelihood that her rapist will be arrested, prosecuted, convicted and sentenced for that crime is well below 1 per cent.

The data and every relevant interest group—with two striking exceptions—agree: our system is not dealing with rape in a way that, on any measure, could legitimately be described as successful. The two exceptions are men's rights groups and some parts of the legal profession, in particular defence lawyers and bar associations, which routinely argue against any law reform that might increase the prospects of success in prosecutions of rape.

The NSW Bar Association is on the record actually opposing the current legal position in that state, arguing, in a submission to the NSW Law Reform Commission in 2018, that 'a person should not be liable to conviction for a sexual assault in circumstances where he or she honestly believes that there is consent'. It was proposing that the possibility of the prosecution securing a conviction, by proving that a defendant who honestly believed there was consent present had no reasonable grounds for holding that belief, should be abolished. That would return us to the law as it was stated in *DPP v Morgan*, whereby non-consent, unless it is verbally and forcibly stated and accompanied by resistance, is irrelevant.

In fairness, as the saying goes, not all barristers. A group of prominent NSW barristers recently stated their public disagreement with the NSW Bar Association's opposition to the freshly announced consent law reforms. As Justin Gleeson SC wrote, quoting his colleague Anthony McGrath SC:

> The traditional approach to the prosecution of sexual assaults has repeatedly failed the victims, who are overwhelmingly women. When we fail the victims of sexual assault, we also fail our community. We need

to address those failings by doing these things differently and better.[21]

I won't go into the reasons why there is such a strong objection in some quarters to fundamental reform of the law of rape, but will say that I can only assume its protagonists are comfortable with the basic proposition that it is better that 100 rapists go free than that one innocent man might face a risk of conviction. It's a legitimate principle to defend—it's just not the hill on which I'd personally choose to die.

But if we know the system is failing, and the very people it is supposedly attempting to serve—survivors—are not clamouring to come under its wing but are in fact mostly avoiding it altogether, or, if they have engaged with it, are coming away more bruised from the experience than they were before they went in, then why is it being maintained? The answer to that question lies in the answer to another question, one which as a society we have not seriously asked.

When I was sitting with Mia as she debriefed her shattering final encounter with Detective Franks, after she had explained how she had been made to feel at the end of all those months of the investigative process—in her words, 'like I was wasting people's time and making it up'—I asked her this question: 'When you made the decision to go to the police and report what had happened to you, what were you seeking?'

Mia replied: 'I didn't necessarily want him to be punished. I wanted to be heard. I wanted to be believed. I wanted for him to be held to account in some way, so that it became real for him too.' She continued: 'I felt I was keeping his secret. Just him being questioned would suffice. I'd be handing the shame and trauma back to him. Handing this shit back to him, so that it was no longer mine. I wanted my agency back, and I didn't want to suffer in silence anymore.'

There is no need for anyone, and it's certainly no right of mine, to editorialise on her words.

～

Mia's reflection will not surprise anyone who has spent time on the field of sexual violence. Grace Tame, in her speech accepting her appointment as 2021 Australian of the Year, said in relation to her own experience of grooming and serial rape by a schoolteacher when she was fifteen: 'Yes, discussion of child sexual abuse is uncomfortable. But nothing is more uncomfortable than the abuse itself. So let us redirect this discomfort to where it belongs: at the feet of perpetrators of these crimes.'[22]

Detective superintendent Maloney put it this way: 'I think most victims want to hear: "I'm really sorry, I shouldn't have made you feel that way" or "I shouldn't have done that".'[23]

When I first started working with survivors, I was surprised by how relatively disinterested, or even uninterested, they seemed to be regarding what we tend to assume would be their primary concern: vindication of their trauma by the public conviction and punishment of their perpetrator. For most survivors, I observed that actually this was presenting as a low-order priority; in some cases it was not on their list at all. Typically, I explore with them their options, which are three (assuming they don't wish to remain silent): a criminal complaint, civil action, or going public with their story. Each pathway is precarious, laden with legal risk and personal cost. What I began to notice was that, almost universally, what survivors were most interested in exploring and understanding wasn't punishment, it wasn't money, and it was never fame or public attention. It was something I'm not sure we've quite identified yet, but if there was a word for it, it would live somewhere between 'agency', 'power', 'autonomy' and 'choice'.

I think this thing connects profoundly to the experience of being raped, something I simply don't and can't understand. I recognise it rationally as the loss of something taken without permission. The key, therefore, to what survivors typically seek when they come to the front door of the legal system, is the restoration of that taken thing. Perhaps it's best described as the restoration of self.

Blue Knot Foundation, the leading national body supporting survivors of childhood trauma, provides guidance for how to talk about trauma with survivors. The principles it articulates as the foundation for every interaction are safety, trustworthiness, choice, collaboration and empowerment.[24] Again, there is nothing here that we don't already know. We have the capacity, evidence and tools to understand what survivors seek and need when they are confronting the trauma of their experience, whether it is recent or happened long ago. We also know in comprehensive detail what the legal system currently offers to them by way of a response. And it is as obvious as anything has ever been that these two things do not match.

Detective superintendent Maloney knows it well:

[After describing how most victims want to hear an apology] But she says the status quo doesn't offer that outcome: instead victim-survivors are usually faced with the choice between an often-gruelling court process or nothing. 'No-one is ever really going to say: "I'm sorry about that, I did it." They're always going to fight it,' Ms Maloney said. 'People admitting guilt to something is difficult. There is a huge stigma attaching to someone who's been convicted of a sexual violence offence. [The] community is quite happy to have more victims than offenders.'[25]

It's true, and we all know it: every woman knows a rape victim, and almost no man knows a rapist. This is insanity.

~

If we were to step back from the wall against which we have been repeatedly banging our heads, far enough to gain some actual perspective, we would realise that we've been having the wrong conversation all along.

We could have arguments from here to eternity about whether the *Crimes Act* should include a statutory definition of 'consent'; whether, if we instituted an affirmative consent model in the law, it would cause a sudden wave of convictions of men who innocently mistook signals for something they weren't.

We could continue to debate up hill and down dale whether it is right or wrong for a defence barrister to be able to ask an alleged rape victim about how much she drank, what she wore, why she was where she was, what she said, what she did, and all the things she didn't do or say, in pursuit of scraping out the hint of a reasonable doubt.

We can go on as we are, telling rape survivors ever more loudly that they should speak up, go to the police, tell their stories and be silenced no more.

But we will do that knowing with absolute certainty that we are asking survivors to submit to being systematically re-traumatised by the process itself, in the name of an end goal that isn't close to any of the things that they most critically want, need and deserve. We will do it knowing that, as soon as survivors do this, their stories will cease to be theirs; that they will personally bear the burden of the case against their rapist, while having no control over it, not even a right to be kept informed; that the man they say raped them will be able to maintain his silence, to never say a word, from the first moment of the process to the last; that, no matter what the outcome is, there is no mechanism in the law that will force him to *take* responsibility for his own actions, as opposed to culpability being imposed upon him.

Why don't survivors report? Why the hell would they?

If we took that step back, however, and saw that we were talking at cross-purposes, then we could stop doing it. If we were to reimagine the legal system's response to rape survivors, then we would start with the needs of the survivors themselves.

As a senior public prosecutor put it to me, we have placed all our eggs in one basket which is not fit for purpose. She knows better than anyone that the criminal justice system she serves was designed, a very long time ago, for crimes that aren't rape.

There are alternatives to what we have. They are well known; they exist in other places. There is a whole world of research and on-the-ground experience from which we can draw.

Detective superintendent Maloney has floated a few ideas herself. Restorative justice is one possibility, a process under which the victim, offender and anyone else affected can be brought together, in a mediated context, to attempt an outcome that looks like what Mia had been seeking all along.

On the criminal culpability side, our slavish devotion to the adversarial system we have inherited, including all the bells and whistles of the prosecutorial burden and the accused's sacrosanct right to silence, blinds us to possible alternative approaches that would have a better chance of securing a conviction rate that makes sense.

That might involve shifting, for crimes of sexual violence, from the adversarial system to an inquisitorial one, in which the focus is not on proof of guilt in a one-sided contest, but on an inquiry whose purpose is to discover the truth. In that context, all parties are obliged to assist. The right to silence, in my personal opinion, should be discarded for crimes of this type. For all the outraged objections, doing so would not be a breach of the rule of law; those who wield that principle as a shield against law reform simply do not understand (or care) what it means.

There are other measures, less terrifying to the reactionary purists, that could still markedly shift the balance. Specialist rape courts are surely a no-brainer. Specialists at every level and phase of the criminal justice process and system would make such a difference: fully trained, trauma-informed, supported by resources dedicated specifically to survivors, and publicly funded, such as independent legal advice, counselling, respite housing and financial support.

Jess Hill, in her documentary series *See What You Made Me Do*, talks about the 'front desk lottery' that domestic and family violence survivors face when they walk into a police station—their experience of the justice system can depend entirely on who happens to be manning the desk.[26] The same applies for rape survivors. It would be silly to expect that all police officers will ever be fully equipped to deal empathically and sensitively with survivors. We should ensure that survivors don't have to play any lottery at all.

Obviously it is not my purpose, and definitely not my place, to propose solutions to the problem of system failure I've raised. What I want to point out is that the failure exists, that it is profound, complete and absolutely known. And I want to affirm that, until we acknowledge the failure of the system we have constructed to respond to survivors of rape, we can guarantee, beyond not just reasonable doubt but all doubt, that we will continue to fail them.

Mia concluded her reflection on her experience of the system in these words: 'The system does the same as the perpetrator: it takes from you until you have no power, no say, and then you're discarded and on the street, shamed and alone.'

We can do better than this.

# ACKNOWLEDGEMENTS

In 2019 I met an extraordinary woman who had decided after thirty years of personal torment to report to the police that she had been raped by a male friend when she was a schoolgirl. Tragically, on 24 June 2020, exactly a year before I completed this work, she took her own life. Her allegation will never be tested in a criminal court.

Her name was Kate and her story is now notorious, not by her choice. I was honoured to know her and by the trust she placed in me, as I have been by each of the many survivors of sexual violence with whom I have worked.

Each of them has left me with the same impressions: that the trauma caused by rape is limitless and for life; that the courage and fortitude required to speak of the experience even in private is enormous, let alone what it takes to do so in any public way; and that what we currently offer to survivors mostly is disillusionment and despair.

I acknowledge each of the women and men who have shared their stories with me, informing my understanding and impressing on me the demand that we urgently move to offer something better. Their names, like their stories, are their possessions.

With thanks to Louise Adler and the team at Monash University Publishing for producing this vital series literally in the national interest; my partners and colleagues at Marque Lawyers who move as one in support of the social justice causes that we consider important; and to Nina Funnell and every-one involved in the advocacy groups End Rape On Campus (EROC) and Rape & Sexual Assault Research & Advocacy (RASARA), all way more knowledgeable than me and tireless in their efforts towards a better system. Finally and always, my family, Charmaine, Sian and Darcy, the lights that guide me.

# NOTES

1   The names of 'Mia' and 'Trent' and the investigating detective
    have been changed to protect their identities. The events
    described are taken from Mia's formal police statements.

2   In June 2021, Stacey Maloney was promoted to an Assistant
    Commissioner (Communications and Security) at the NSW
    Police Force.

3   Natassia Chrysanthos, '"Admitting Guilt Is Difficult": How Sex
    Crimes Boss Wants the Justice System to Change', *The Sydney
    Morning Herald*, 28 April 2021.

4   According to the most recent Australian Bureau of Statistics
    data, from 2016, in 87 per cent of cases of a woman's most recent
    incident of sexual assault by a male, the perpetrator was known
    to her: Australian Bureau of Statistics, *Personal Safety, Australia,
    2016*, ABS cat. no. 4906.0, 2017.

5   Online Etymology Dictionary, 'rape (v.)', 2021, https://www.
    etymonline.com/word/rape (viewed June 2021).

6   Germaine Greer, *On Rape*, Hachette Australia, Sydney, 2020.

7   *DPP v Morgan* [1976] A.C. 182; 214.

8   Judith Herman, 'Justice from the Victim's Perspective', vol. 11,
    no. 5, *Violence against Women*, 2005, pp. 571–602.

9   Victorian Law Reform Commission, *Victims of Crime
    in the Criminal Trial Process: Report*, Melbourne, 2016,
    recommendation no. 23.

10  In May 2021, the NSW attorney-general announced that he
    would be moving to amend this last provision so that an alleged
    rape defendant will not be able to access the 'reasonable grounds'
    escape clause if he did not take positive steps to ascertain

consent. This will help the prosecution, but it is not (as it has been widely described) an affirmative consent model.

11  The names of 'Dina' and 'Terry' have been changed to protect their identities.

12  Louise Milligan, *Witness*, Hachette Australia, Sydney, 2020.

13  *Lazarus v R* [2016] NSWCCA 52, [75].

14  *R v Lazarus*, District Court of New South Wales, Judgment of Tupman DCJ, 4 May 2017, pp. 41, 60.

15  Ibid., p. 72.

16  Judith Herman, *Trauma and Recovery: The Aftermath of Violence—From Domestic Abuse to Political Terror*, Basic Books, New York, 2015.

17  Rape & Domestic Violence Services Australia, *Submission to the NSW Law Reform Commission Review of Consent in Relation to Sexual Offences*, 29 June 2018.

18  Angus Thompson, '"I Hope Justice Systems Change": NSW Police Commissioner Wants Rape Law Reform', *The Sydney Morning Herald*, 12 March 2021.

19  Ibid.

20  Australian Bureau of Statistics, *Personal Safety, Australia, 2016*, ABS cat. no. 4906.0, 2017.

21  Justin Gleeson, 'Sexual Consent Reforms Will Bring Laws into Line with Community Standards', *The Sydney Morning Herald*, 3 June 2021.

22  ABC News, '"Hear Me Now": Australian of the Year Grace Tame's Speech in Full', 26 January 2021.

23  Natassia Chrysanthos, '"Admitting Guilt Is Difficult": How Sex Crimes Boss Wants the Justice System to Change', *The Sydney Morning Herald*, 28 April 2021.

24  Dr Cathy Kezelman and Pam Stavropoulos, *Talking about Trauma: Guide to Everyday Conversations for the General Public*, Blue Knot Foundation, Sydney, 2017.

25  Natassia Chrysanthos, '"Admitting Guilt Is Difficult": How Sex Crimes Boss Wants the Justice System to Change', *The Sydney Morning Herald*, 28 April 2021.

26  SBS, *See What You Made Me Do*, 2021.